R. White

Whites Excelsior Method for the Banjo

Without a teacher

R. White

Whites Excelsior Method for the Banjo
Without a teacher

ISBN/EAN: 9783741115295

Manufactured in Europe, USA, Canada, Australia, Japa

Cover: Foto ©Angelika Wolter / pixelio.de

Manufactured and distributed by brebook publishing software (www.brebook.com)

R. White

Whites Excelsior Method for the Banjo

R. White

Whites Excelsior Method for the Banjo

CONTENTS.

INSTRUCTION.

	PAGE
Elements of Music	3
Notes, Rests and the Staff	3
The Clef	4
Time, Measure and Bar	5
Accidentals	5
Scales, Major and Minor	5
The Chromatic Scale	7, 16, 17, and 21
Miscellaneous Characters	7
Ornaments, Appogiaturas, Gruppetto (or Turn)	8
The Trill, (or Shake)	9
Tremolo, Arpeggios and other signs	10
The Banjo (descriptive diagram,) Strings, Bridge, etc.	11
How to tune the Banjo	11
Holding the Banjo, Position of the Hands and Arms	12

	PAGE
Playing the Banjo. Fingers of the right and left hand.	1
Diagrams illustrating the preceding rules	13 and 1
The Positions, Barre, Touch, Chords, Arpeggios and Harmonic Tones	1
Fingerboard of the Banjo	16 and 1
Scales	18 and 2
Scale of A major with chords and fingerings	1
" E "	1
" D "	1
" G "	2
" F sharp minor "	2
" A minor "	2
System of Double Fingering	2
The Tremolo	8

COMPOSITIONS.

	PAGE
Arkansas Traveller	31
Alabama Wing Dance	39
Andalucia (Valse Espagnole)	78
Banjoists' Favorite	31
Banjo Caprice	39
Banjo Dance (Polka Comique)	48
Bolero Mexicana	63
Chappies' Polka	45
Chopsticks (Chinese March)	27
Clayton's Grand March	66
Col. Goetting's March	56
Dancing on the Meadow	52
Den Thompson's Reel	33
Down in Dixie Polka	36
Dreamy Eyes Waltz	34
Easter Lilies Waltz	57
Fancy Dance	24
Fisher's Hornpipe	29
Fisherman and his child, The.	51
Golden Bird Polka	68
"Growler" Hornpipe	27
Guardmount (The German patrol)	60
I met her at the Ball	62
Jean Missud's March	50
Jolly Dude Schottische	40
Josh Whitcomb's Reel	33
Kiss Waltz	38
Last Rose of Summer	65
L'Etoile D'Affection Mazurka	28
Let the Band Play. (Grand Marche de Ballet)	58

	PAGE
Little Beauty Schottische	2
Little Beauty Waltz	2
Little Fairy Schottische	4
Maid on the Green. (Irish Jig.)	2
Marguerite. (Romanza)	6
Money Musk	4
My Love. (Caprice)	2
On Deck Hornpipe	3
Original Heel and Toe Polka	4
Pizzicati (Sylvia)	6
Razzle Dazzle Clog	3
Ribbon Polka	4
Run of Luck	5
Said Pasha Schottische	5
Scotch Reel	2
Shoo! Fly, Don't bother me	2
Silver Heels Clog	2
Skipping Rope Schottische	4
Standard Bearer March	7
Star of affection Mazurka	2
Summer days Waltz	5
The Tipsy Tailor. (Old Irish Jig)	7
Tom-Tom Polka	7
Twinkle, Twinkle Little Star	4
Waltz Medley	7
Waves of the ocean (Galop)	4
Wild Flower Schottische	3
Wing Dance	2
York, The.	3

ELEMENTS OF MUSIC.

The principal characters used to express music are NOTES, which represent musical sounds, and RESTS, which represent silence.

These characters are written upon the STAFF, a union of 5 lines and the 4 spaces between.

THE STAFF.

NOTES AND RESTS.

The different kinds and their names.

NOTES.

Whole note. Half note. Quarter note. Eighth note. Sixteenth note. Thirty-second note. Sixty-fourth note.

RESTS.

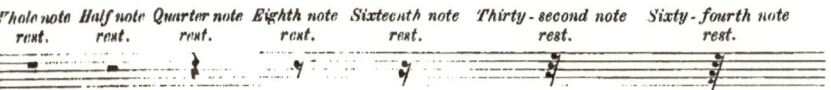

Whole note rest. Half note rest. Quarter note rest. Eighth note rest. Sixteenth note rest. Thirty-second note rest. Sixty-fourth note rest.

Table showing the relative time-value of notes.

A Whole note is equal in time-value to
2 Half notes
or
4 Quarter notes
or
8 Eigth notes
or
16 Sixteenth notes
or
32 Thirty-second notes
(or 64 Sixty-fourth notes.)

The same rule applies also to the Rests.

DOTTED NOTES AND RESTS.

A Dot after a note or rest increases the time-value one half.

Dotted Notes and Rests and their Equivalents.

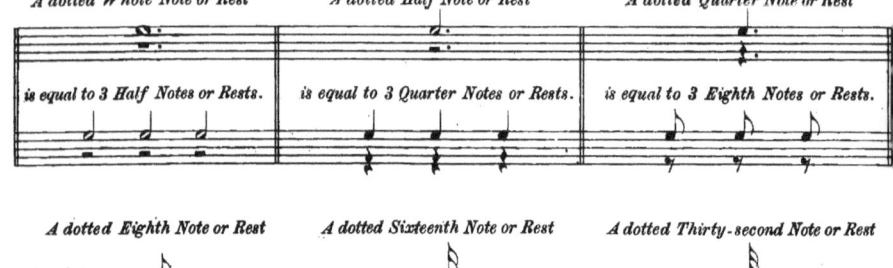

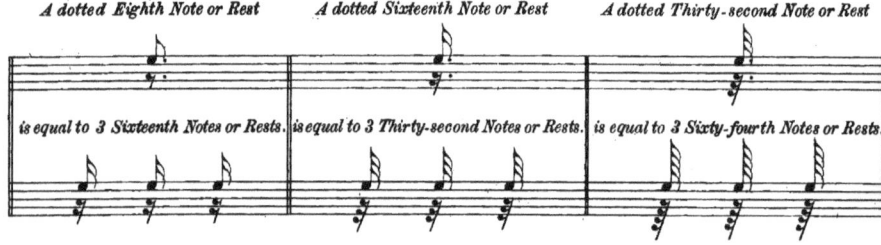

A *second dot* after a note or rest adds to the time-value of the note or rest, one half the value of the *first dot*. Thus a double-dotted Half Note (𝅗𝅥··) is equal to 3 Quarter Notes and 1 Eighth Note (♩ ♩ ♩ ♪), and a double-dotted Quarter Note (♩··) to 3 Eighth Notes and 1 Sixteenth Note(♪ ♪ ♪ ♬) and so on. Double dotted Rests have the same relative time-values as corresponding notes.

THE CLEF.

The CLEF is a character usually placed at the beginning of the Staff to indicate the Musical Pitch of the notes written thereon.

For all the higher instruments such as the FLUTE, VIOLIN, OBOE, CLARINET, CORNET, HORN, GUITAR, MANDOLIN and also the BANJO, FLAGEOLET, FIFE, CONCERTINA, ACCORDEON and some others, a Clef called the G Clef is used. It fixes the tone G upon the 2d line of the Staff.

G Clef. 𝄞 or Treble Clef.

For instruments of a lower compass such as the VIOLONCELLO, DOUBLE BASS, BASSOON, TROMBONE, TUBA and others, a Clef called the F Clef is used. It fixes F upon the 4th line of the Staff.

F Clef. 𝄢 or Bass Clef.

A Clef called the C Clef is used especially for the VIOLA and fixes C upon the middle line of the Staff. This is called the Alto Clef. When placed on the 4th line it is called the Tenor Clef.

ALTO CLEF. TENOR CLEF.   TREBLE CLEF. BASS CLEF.

C Clef. 𝄡 𝄡 Same pitch as 𝄞 or 𝄢

In Music for the Violoncello, Bassoon and some others, several of these clefs are sometimes used.

Music for the PIANO, ORGAN and HARP requires the use of both the G and the F Clefs, which are placed on separate Staves connected by what is called a BRACE.

EX.

TIME, MEASURE & BAR.

There are three kinds of Time, viz: — *Common, Triple & Compound* Time.

Examples of Common Time. | Examples of Triple Time. | Examples of Compound Time.

C or 4/4,   2/4,   ₵ or 2/2   3/4,   3/2,   3/8   6/8,   9/8,   12/8,   6/4

The lower of the two figures indicates the kind of a note, and the upper, how many of that kind of a note are contained in a measure. Thus, 3/4 indicates that there are three quarter notes to a measure.

A MEASURE is that portion of a musical composition contained between two single bars. A BAR is a perpendicular line drawn through the staff, thus: ≡ A DOUBLE BAR ≡ is placed at the end of a piece of music; sometimes at the end of a section (strain) thereof. A DOUBLE BAR with dots, thus: ≡ is called a repeat, and signifies a repetition from the previous double bar, or the commencement of the piece.

ACCIDENTALS.

The Sharp (♯), Flat (♭), Natural (♮), Double Sharp (𝄪) and Double Flat (♭♭) are called ACCIDENTALS.
The ♯ before a note *raises* it a Semitone (half tone).   The ♭ before a note *lowers* it a Semitone.
The 𝄪 "   "   "   "   "   "   Whole Tone.   The ♭♭ "   "   "   "   "   "   Whole Tone.
The ♮ before a note removes a previous ♯ or ♭.
The ♮♯ before a note that has been double-sharped *lowers* it a Semitone.
The ♮♭ "   "   "   "   "   "   double-flatted *raises* " "   "
The Sharps and Flats placed next to the Clef are called the *Signature*. EX.   or

NOTE.— Each Sharp or Flat in the Signature affects that particular tone upon which it is placed so long as it remains in the Signature, unless changed by the introduction of other accidentals before the notes.

THE SCALE.

A SCALE is a series of Musical sounds, ascending or descending according to a system of tones and semitones. The first seven letters of the Alphabet are applied to the seven principal tones of the Scale. Also the Italian monosyllables *Do Re Mi Fa Sol La Si*.

It has already been shown that the G Clef fixes G upon the 2d line of the Staff. From this starting point all other tones can be determined. Notes extending above or below the regular degrees of the Staff are written upon what are called LEDGER LINES, and the spaces between.

EX.

NOTE. Observe that the seven letters follow each other in regular alphabetical order, and that the eighth letter is always the same as the first, whichever one we begin with. It is therefore said to be an *Octave* (8 tones) higher or lower than the first, accordingly as we go up or down.

DIFFERENT KINDS OF SCALES.

The Scale is the basis of all music. There are three kinds in common use: the *Major Scale*, the *Minor Scale*, and the *Chromatic Scale*. The *Major Scale* consists of seven principal tones, viz: five whole tones, and two semitones. The semitones occur between the *third* and *fourth*, and the *seventh* and *eighth* degrees of the Scale. Degrees or intervals may be *Major, Minor,* or *Perfect*, viz;— Major 2d, Minor 2d, Major 3d, Minor 3d, Perfect 4th, Perfect 5th, and so on up to the octaves.

The Major Scale.

SCALE OF C MAJOR.

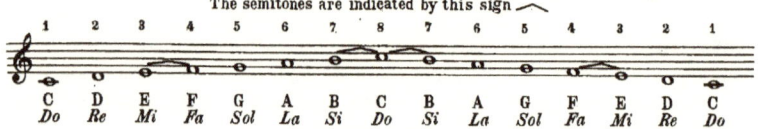

All Major Scales have the same construction and the same order of intervals, ascending or descending.

The Minor Scale.

Every *Major Scale* has its relative *Minor*. The *Signature* is the same in each, and the Key-note is a *Minor Third* (tone and a half) below that of the relative Major Scale. Ex. It has also five tones and two semitones, but with a difference in the order of intervals. The semitones occur between the *second* and *third*, and *seventh* and *eighth* degrees of the scale *ascending*, and between the *fifth* and *sixth* and *second* and *third* degrees *descending*.

SCALE OF A MINOR. (Relative to C Major.)

There are two kinds of Minor Scales in common use; the above which is called the *Melodic Minor Scale*, and the following which is called the *Harmonic Minor Scale*. Observe the difference in the arrangement of the semitones.

SCALE OF A MINOR.

As the Student will meet both forms in his subsequent practice, an example of each has therefore been given.

THE CHROMATIC SCALE.

This Scale is composed of twelve semitones, and may be formed upon any degree of the scale, major or minor. In *ascending*, the Sharp, Double-sharp, or Natural is employed in its formation, but in *descending*, the Flat, Double-flat, or Natural is used accordingly as there are sharps or flats in the signature.

MISCELLANEOUS CHARACTERS

Notes having a dot or dash over or under them are to be played short and detached. This is called *Staccato*.

This sign ⌢ called a *Hold*, placed over a note or rest, prolongs it beyond its exact value. It is sometimes placed at the end of a piece instead of the word *Fine*, which means the end.

The character ⌢ called a *Tie* when placed over two notes on the *same degree of the staff* ⌢ makes them one continuous sound.

When placed over two notes on *different degrees* it is called a *Slur* and indicates that the notes it applies to are to be played in a smooth and connected manner.

Three notes played in the time of two of the same kind are called a *Triplet*, and are indicated thus: A *Sextolet* is a group of six notes played in the time of four of the same kind. EX.

The 𝄋 called a *Sign*, directs the player back to where it was previously indicated, for the purpose of repeating a certain portion of the music.

A passage that repeats, sometimes has two endings indicated thus: That marked ⌐1°⌐ is to be played the first time and the other ⌐2°⌐ the second time.

Every measure has its natural or primary and secondary accents, besides other smaller subdivisions. When the natural accent is perverted and made to fall on an unaccented division of the measure it is called *Syncopation*.

When a stronger accent is required than that which naturally belongs to a note it is indicated by one or another of the following signs called *Accent Marks*. ∧, > or *fz* called *Forzando*, *rfz Rinforzando*, and sometimes *ffz*, according to the degree of accent desired.

When a group of notes or a measure that is to be repeated, is written like the following, it is called *Abbreviation*.

ORNAMENTS.

The chief musical embellishments are the *Appoggiatura* (or Grace Note), the *Gruppetto* (or Turn), and the *Trill* (or Shake).

APPOGGIATURAS.

The Appoggiatura is a small note placed before a principal note for the purpose of ornamentation or effect. There are two kinds of Appoggiaturas in common use — the *Long* Appoggiatura, which takes one half of the time-value of the principal note before which it is placed and also receives the accent — and the *Short* Appoggiatura, which is played very quickly, the accent in this case falling on the principal note.

A group of Appoggiatura notes sometimes precedes a principal note. These notes are played very rapidly and the principal note receives the accent.

and other forms.

THE GRUPPETTO (or Turn).

This musical embellishment is a group of notes (3 or 4, as the case may be) consisting of a principal note and the next note above and below it. It is indicated by the sign ∞. There are several forms of the Gruppetto as will be seen by the following examples.

Examples of the Gruppetto.

When a note in the Gruppetto is to be sharped or flatted, either above or below the principal note, or both, the sign is expressed accordingly, in the following manner:

THE TRILL (or Shake).

The Trill is a rapid alternation of two notes a tone or a semitone apart. It is indicated by the sign *tr* placed above the principal note, the alternating note being the one next above it.* There are three kinds of trills — the *Perfect Trill*, (with finishing notes) — the *Imperfect Trill*, (without finishing notes) — and the *Mordente* or short trill, indicated thus ⁓.

*Sometimes the next one *below* it.

Examples of the Trill.

Perfect Trill.

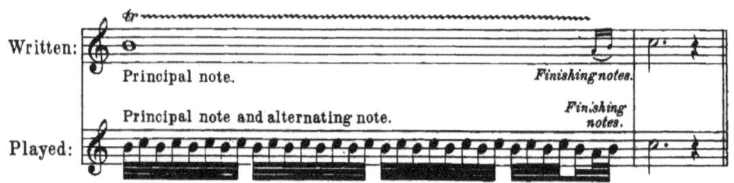

Imperfect Trill.

Mordente (or Short Trill).

OTHER SIGNS.

Tremolo.

A very rapid repetition of the same tone is called *Tremolo.*

Arpeggios.

When chords are to be played in the manner of the Harp it is called *Arpeggio.*

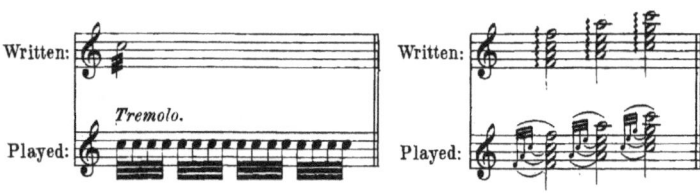

p, piano	means	soft.
pp, pianissimo	"	very soft.
f, forte	"	loud.
ff, fortissimo	"	very loud.
mf, mezzo-forte	"	half or moderately loud.
fp, forte-piano	"	loud and immediately soft again.
fz, sf or >, *sforzando*	"	sharply accented.
crescendo, cresc. or ————	"	increasing in loudness.
diminuendo, dim. or ————	"	decreasing in loudness.

WHITE'S EXCELSIOR METHOD
FOR THE
BANJO.

DESCRIPTIVE DIAGRAM OF THE BANJO.

A, the Banjo Head. B, the Bridge. 1,2,3,4,5, the Strings. C, the Rim. D, the Hoop. E, the Hooks and Brackets around the Hoop and Rim. F, the Stringholder. H, the Peg-Head. I, the Pegs. K, the Nut. L, the Fingerboard. M, Inlaid ornaments indicating Positions 5, 7, 9, 11, etc. N, the Frets. O, the Neck.

THE STRINGS AND BRIDGE.

The five strings of the Banjo are the 1st string, (B); the 2d string, (G#); the 3d string, (E); the 4th string, (A); the 5th string, (E). The 1st and 5th, both B strings, are the same size; the 2d string is a grade larger, and the 3d string a grade larger still. The 4th string is made of white silk, wound with silver wire. The Bridge over which the strings pass to the Pegs, should stand at exactly the same distance from the 12th fret, that the latter stands from the Nut.

THE STRINGS.

HOW TO TUNE THE BANJO.

First tune the 4th string by means of a pitch-pipe, piano, or other instrument to A, as shown in the diagram above. Then place the second finger on the seventh fret of the 4th string, and tune the 3d string in unison with it, producing E. Next, place the second finger on the 3d string, at the fourth fret and tune the 2d string in unison with it, producing G#. Next, place the second finger on the third fret of the 2d string, and tune the 1st string in unison with it, producing B. Lastly, place the second finger on the fifth fret of the 1st string, and tune the 5th string in unison with it, producing E, an octave above the 3d string.

This is the standard mode of tuning the Banjo as regards intervals; but it is now the almost universal custom to raise the pitch of all the strings a minor third higher. When thus tuned the strings sound as follows:

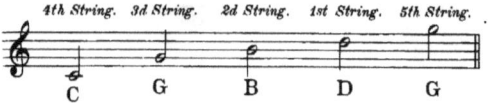

        C   G   B   D   G

This manner of tuning renders the tone of the Banjo much more brilliant. The music, however the instrument may be tuned, is always to be played in the regular manner.

HOLDING THE BANJO.

The banjoist should always sit in an easy and graceful position, the left foot resting naturally on the floor, the heel of the right slightly raised from the ball of the foot, with the hoop of the banjo resting on the right thigh, and so near to the body that the instrument can be kept in place by a moderate but firm pressure of the right breast upon the upper part of the banjo-head.

Support the neck of the banjo (which should incline somewhat towards the left) in the hollow between the thumb and the largest joint of the forefinger of the left hand, the thumb being on the upper side of the neck, next to the bass string, between the nut and the first fret, with the first and second fingers directly over the 2d and 1st strings.

POSITION OF THE HANDS AND ARMS.

The left hand should press the neck of the banjo lightly but firmly, and, when required, glide smoothly and flexibly up and down the fingerboard.

The left arm must not be constrained, but should slope gradually away from the shoulder, the elbow being kept at a little distance from the body.

The right arm should rest lightly on the rim, with the right hand just in front of the bridge. Place the little finger lightly on the banjo-head to support and steady it, but do not allow it to restrict in the least, the action of the other fingers.

PLAYING THE BANJO.

The Fingers of the Right Hand.

As a rule, apply the first finger to the 2d string, and the second finger to the 1st string. The 3d, 4th, and 5th strings are played with the thumb. Pick the 1st and 2d strings upwards, and the 3d, 4th, and 5th strings downwards. The third finger is not used except in chords and arpeggios.

The Fingers of the Left Hand.

The fingers of the left hand are indicated by the following figures: First finger,   1.
        Second finger,   2.   Third finger,   3.
        Fourth finger,   4.   The open strings, o.

Notes to be struck with the thumb +. The 5th string is usually indicated by a character called the *flag*; thus:

THE POSITIONS, BARRE, TOUCH, &c.

When the first finger is placed at the 1st fret, the hand is said to be in the 1st Position. There are 24 positions on the Banjo. The Barre is made by placing the first finger of the left hand with a firm pressure directly across the strings, at any fret, and by raising the wrist somewhat, and pressing the thumb firmly against the under side of the neck of the Banjo, keeping the other fingers free to stop the strings when required. A good tone is always a prime requisite. To obtain this on the Banjo, touch the strings with the fleshy part of the fingers only, and carefully avoid any contact with them of the nails, as it produces a snappy, unmusical sound. The fingers of the left hand should be placed very close to the frets, and the strings pressed down with firmness and flexibility. This will ensure a full, clear musical tone.

Example.

CHORDS AND ARPEGGIOS.

A chord is a combination of three or more tones sounded simultaneously.

Chords.

Arpeggios.

When the intervals of a chord are sounded successively it is called *Arpeggio*. In playing arpeggios place all the fingers of the left hand at once on the stopped notes of the chord that is to be played, and keep them down firmly until a change of fingering occurs. This ensures good vibration. The fingers of the right hand should not touch the strings except to sound the notes that are to be played. In executing arpeggios of four and five notes, place the first finger on the 3d string, the second finger on the 2d string, and the third finger on the 1st string; the thumb having special control of the 4th and 5th strings. Strike the tones from the lowest upwards. Sign of the arpeggio {

Arpeggios.

Written
Played

Harmonic Tones.

By placing the finger lightly on a string at any one of the frets, a tone called *harmonic* can be produced. The best harmonic tones are obtained at the fourth, fifth, seventh, twelfth, twentieth and twenty-fourth frets on the 1st, 2d, 3d and 4th strings, and also at the seventeenth fret on the 5th string.

The finger of the left hand must press the string just enough to prevent its vibrating as if open, while at the same time a refined touch is also necessary with the fingers of the right hand.

FINGERBOARD OF THE BANJO.

The following diagram shows all the tones of the Banjo in the form of the Chromatic Scale ascending by sharps.

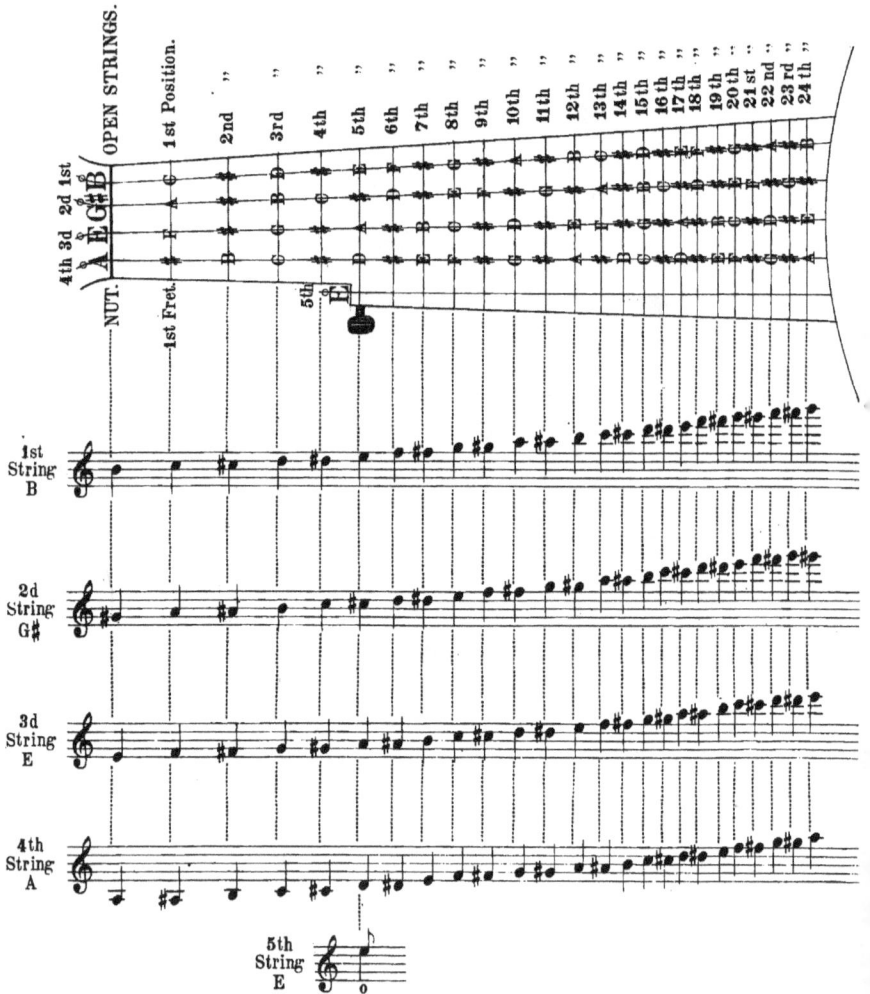

FINGERBOARD OF THE BANJO.

The following diagram shows all the tones of the Banjo in the form of a Chromatic Scale descending by flats.

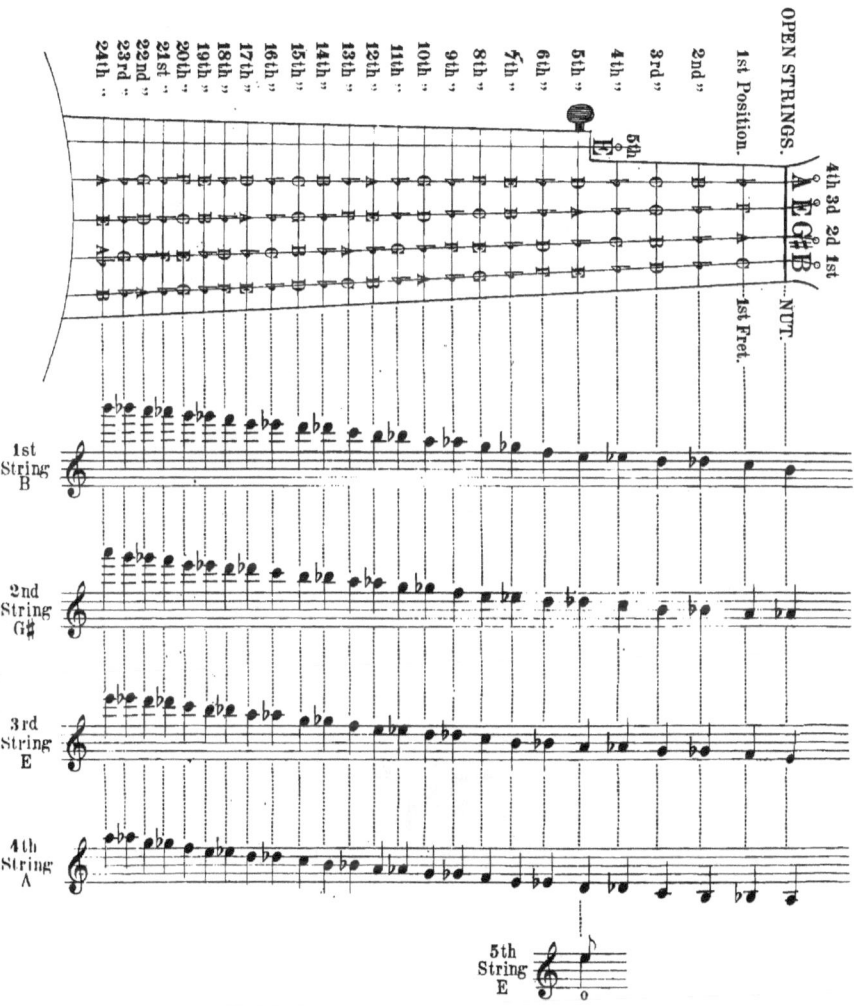

SCALES.

Although the modern Banjo may be played in all the keys, major and minor, still there are certain keys peculiar to the instrument which are almost exclusively used in music written or arranged for it. The keys principally employed are those of A major, (called the natural key of the Banjo) E major, D major and G major. Also the keys of F# minor and A minor. The key of C major and the flat keys are rarely used on account of the greater difficulties of fingering which they present, and the very frequent use of the barre which they require. The following diagrams exemplify the most useful and practical keys with their scales and simple harmonies.

The student is advised to acquire a perfect knowledge of each scale and its accompanying chords before attempting to play any of the selections in that key, which the book contains further on.

Key of A major.

Scale and Chords with Fingerings.

Scale.

Fingering for the Left Hand.

Chords.

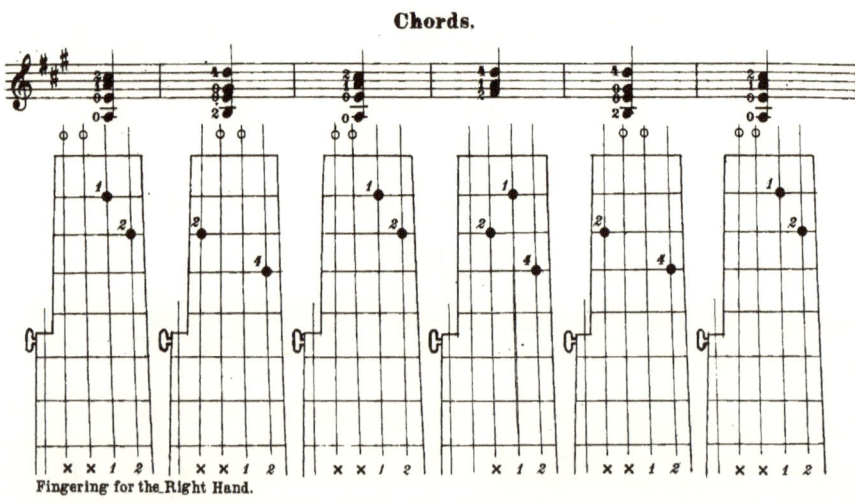

Fingering for the Right Hand.

Key of E Major.
Scale.

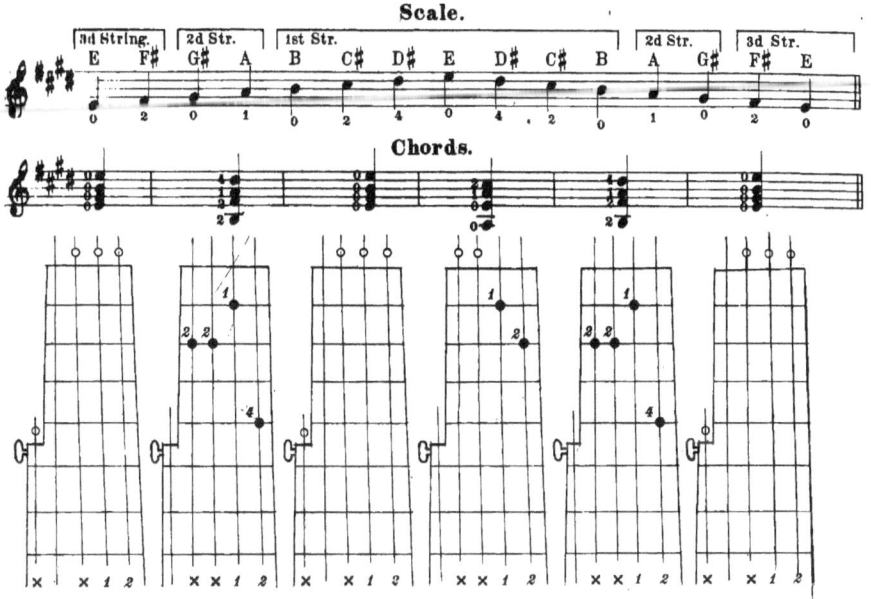

Chords.

Key of D Major.
Scale.

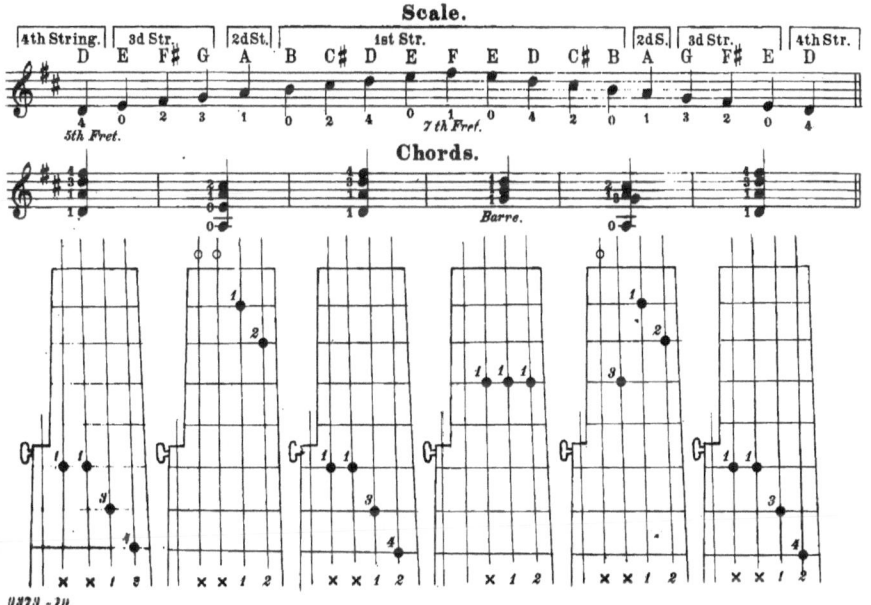

Chords.

Key of G Major.

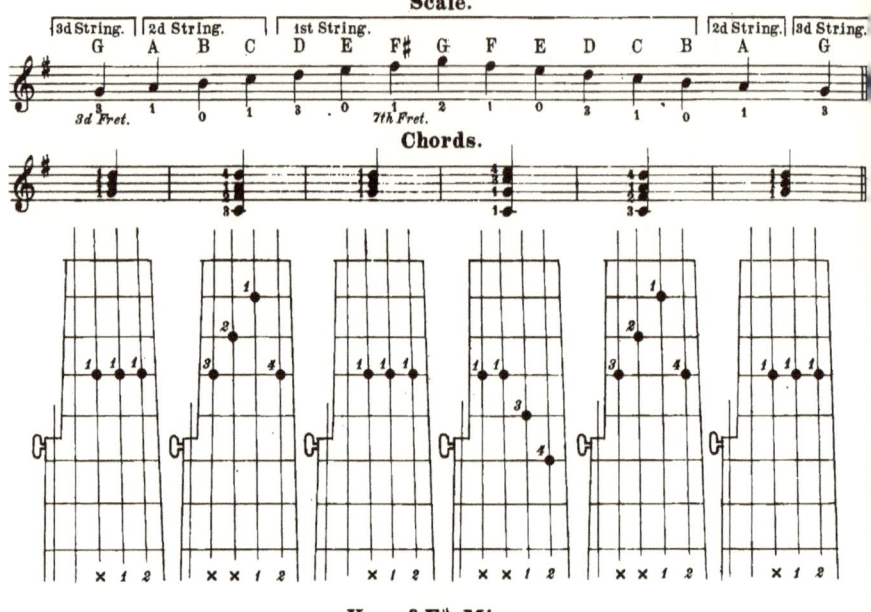

Key of F# Minor.

21

Key of A Minor.

Scale.

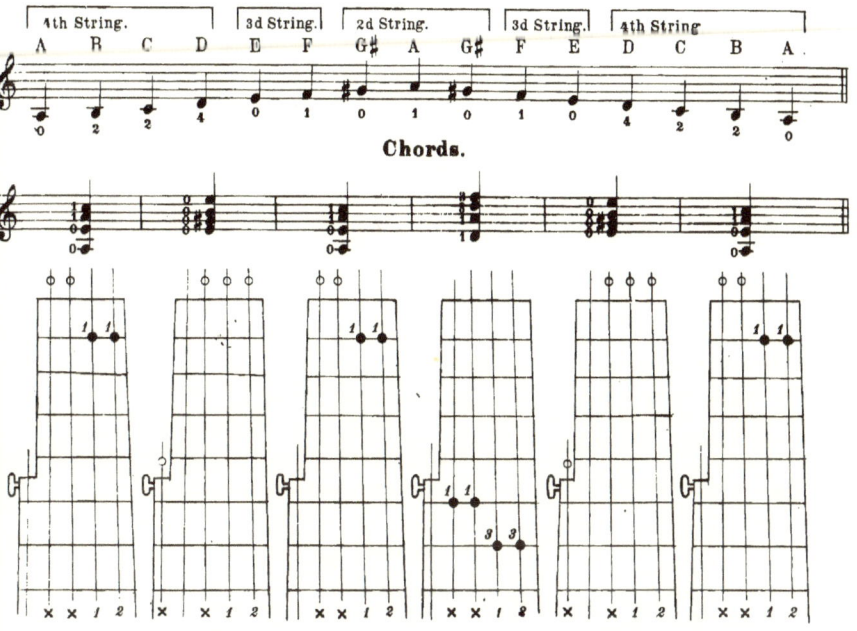

CHROMATIC SCALE.

As has already been shown on page 7, (see also diagram, pages 16 and 17) the Chromatic Scale is composed of a regular succession of semitones and may be formed on any interval of the scale, major or minor. The following example with fingering which begins with the lowest open string of the Banjo will serve as a practical example in general of this scale.

System of Double Fingering.

The Banjo as now played is capable of wonderful execution. The system of double fingering enables the player to perform rapid passages which a few years ago were considered impossible.

Example.

Some performers write the scale fingering starting with the thumb. It is better, however, to start the scale as above, inasmuch as it leaves the proper finger ready for each succeeding open string.

The system as given in the above example is used by the leading players.

Exercises
showing when to start with the first finger and when to start with the thumb.

Examples.

SCALES.

The following scales with the fingerings marked are all that the banjoist will be likely to meet with in ordinary practise. Should any of the more remote keys present themselves, apply the same general system of fingering in playing them, as in those previously learned. Observe that the same signature is employed to indicate both the major key and its relative minor.

Besides the above there are also the following major and minor keys.

B major.   F# major.   C# major.   Db major.   Gb major.   Cb major.
                                    and
G# minor. D# minor.   A# minor.   Bb minor.   Eb minor.   Ab minor.

ON DECK HORNPIPE.

BART FOLEY.

SILVER HEELS CLOG.

DAVE BRAMAN.

THE TIPSY TAILOR.

Old Irish Jig.

CHOP STICKS.
(CHINESE MARCH.)

WUN LUNG.

"THE GROWLER" HORNPIPE.

4th String Elevated.

DAVE BRAMAN.

MAID ON THE GREEN.

4th String Elevated.

Irish Jig.

L'ETOILE D'AFFECTION.
(STAR OF AFFECTION.)
MAZURKA.

HARTMAN.

SHEW! FLY, DON'T BOTHER ME.

CAMPBELL.

FISHER'S HORNPIPE.

4th String Elevated.

THE YORK.
(ONE HEART, ONE SOUL.)

JOH. STRAUSS.

WILD FLOWER.
(SCHOTTISCHE.)

C. A. WHITE.

RUN OF LUCK.
(SCHOTTISCHE.)

Tune 4th to B.

CHAS. D. BLAKE.

DOWN IN DIXIE.
(POLKA.)

C. A. WHITE.

JOLLY DUDE SCHOTTISCHE.

GEO. THORNE.

LITTLE FAIRY SCHOTTISCHE.

STREABBOG.

TRIO.

ORIGINAL HEEL AND TOE POLKA.

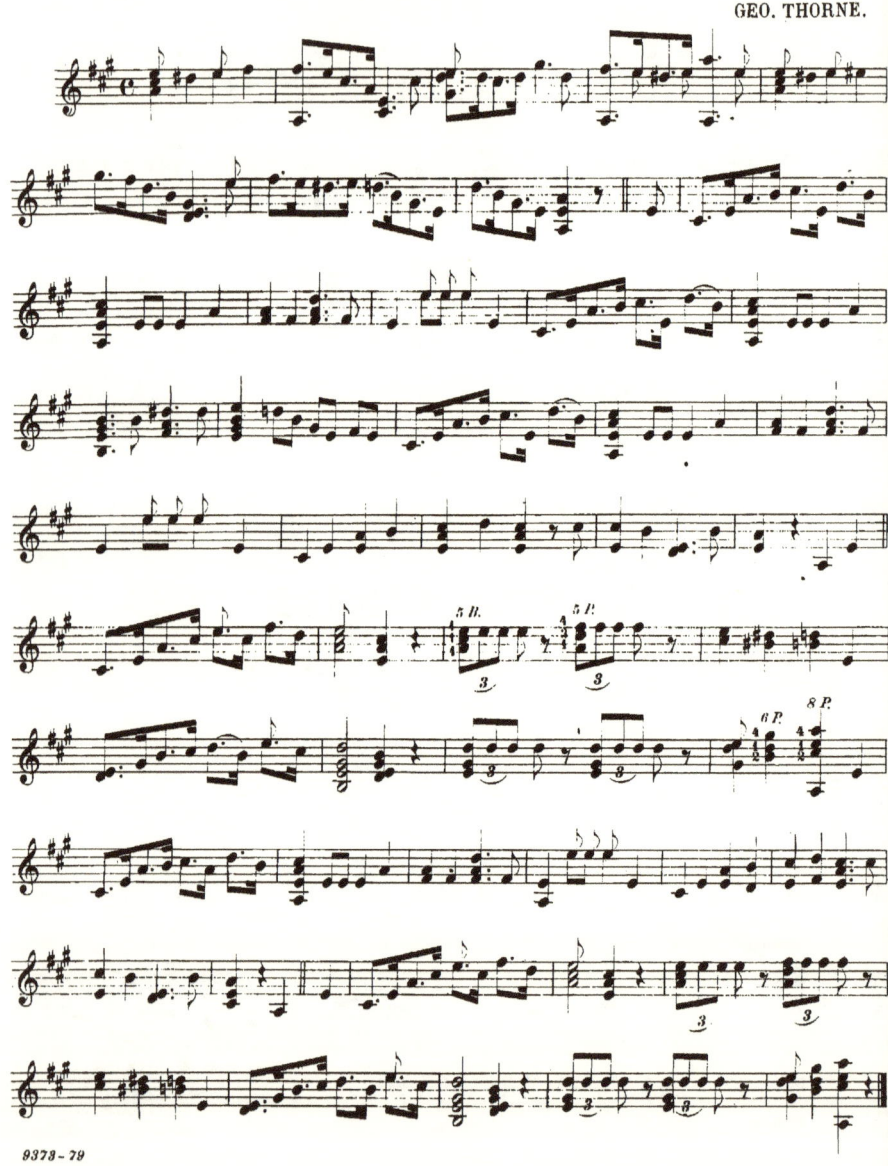

WAVES OF THE OCEAN.
(GALOP.)
CHAS. D. BLAKE.

SKIPPING ROPE SCHOTTISCHE.

4th String Elevated.

C. D. BLAKE.

CHAPPIES POLKA.

Elevate Bass String. FLORENCE FARE.

MY LOVE.
(CAPRICE.)
C. M. ZIEHRER.

JEAN MISSUDS MARCH.

4th String Elevated.

W. R. HOSMER.

Marcato.

Signifies 4th String.

D.C. al Fine.

THE FISHERMAN AND HIS CHILD.

C. A. WHITE.

DANCING ON THE MEADOW.

C. D. BLAKE.

F. E. WHITE.

* The Drum parts may be produced by tapping on the Banjo Head.

D.C. al Fine.

LET THE BAND PLAY.
(GRANDE MARCHE DE BALLET.)

F. E. WHITE.

SAID PASHA.
(SCHOTTISCHE.)
GEO. THORNE.

Tune 4th to B.
D. L. WHITE.

BOLERO MEXICANA.

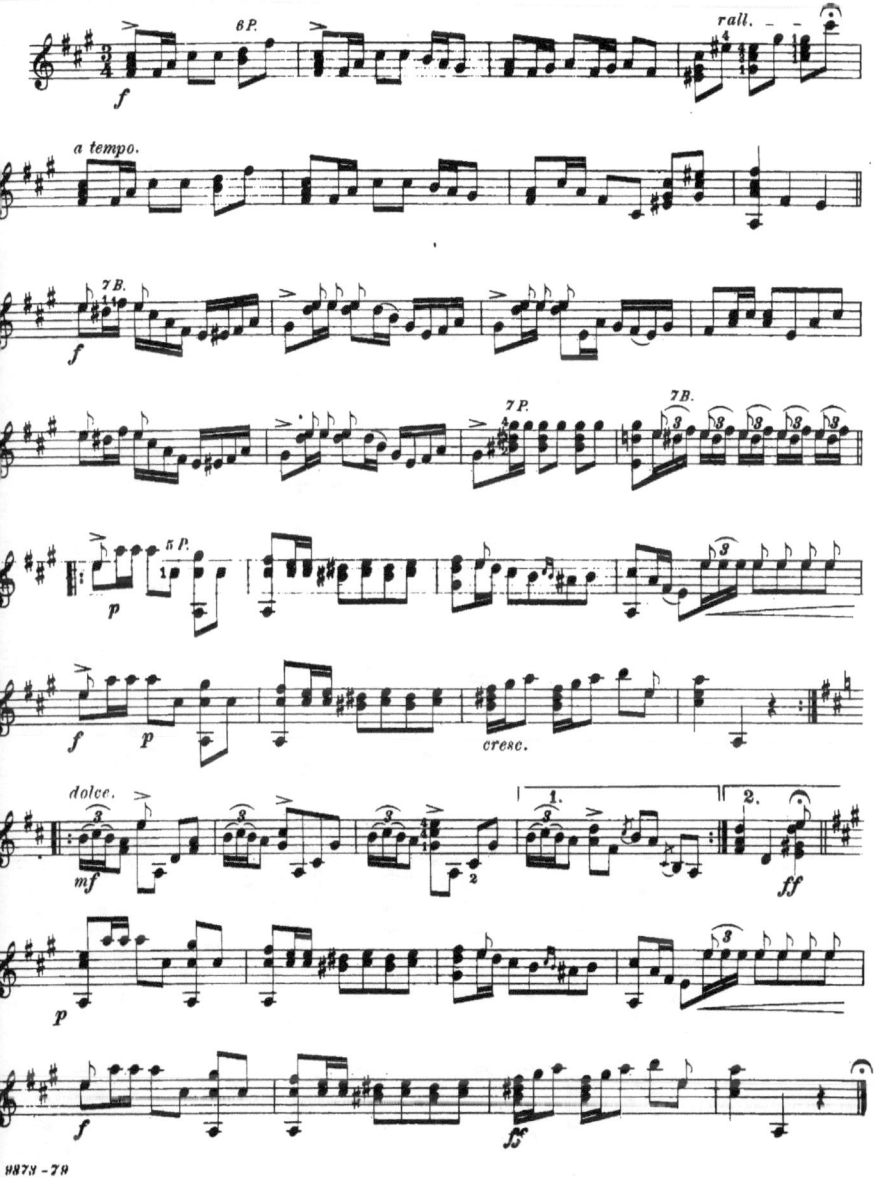

PIZZICATI
(From Ballet - "SYLVIA.")

LEO DELIBES.

GOLDEN BIRD POLKA.

INTRO. **Andante.** Trem.

NARCISSE BOUSQUET.
Arr. by G. L. Lansing.

STANDARD BEARER MARCH.

1st Banjo Elevate Bass String.

PHILLIPP FAHRBACH, Jr.

73

74

WALTZ MEDLEY.

Arr. by G. L. LANSING.

*A figure in a circle ③ signifies the string.

ANDALUCIA.
(VALSE ESPAGNOLE.)

Le THIERE.

✱ When played as a duett small notes may be omitted.

THE TREMOLO.

The Tremolo movement is the nearest approach to a sustained tone possible on the Banjo. When artistically performed it is very effective.

In playing Tremolo, rest the third finger of the right hand on the head about three inches from the bridge, elevate the hand so that only the point of the first finger will touch the strings.

The motion of the first finger should be forward and backward very fast on one, two or three strings according to the number of notes written.

The notes with stems turned up are made tremolo, those turned down are all picked with the thumb as an accompaniment.

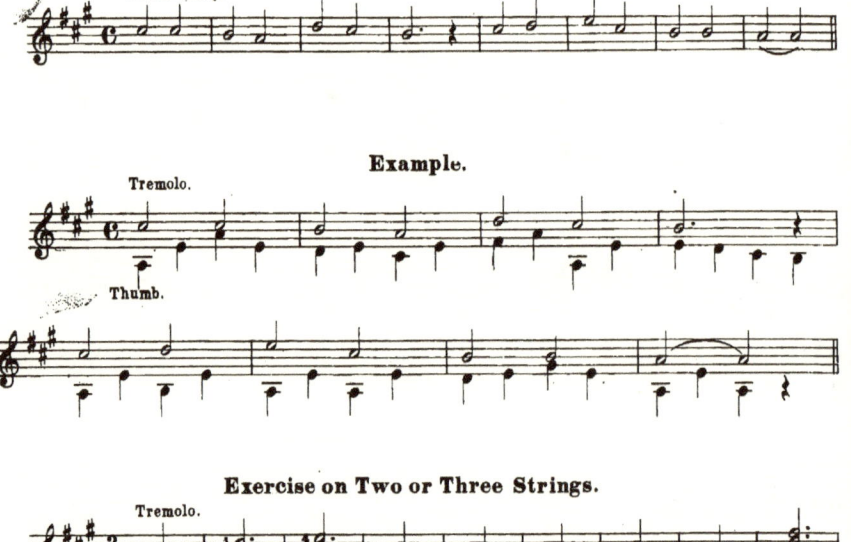

www.ingramcontent.com/pod-product-compliance
Lightning Source LLC
Chambersburg PA
CBHW020332090426
42735CB00009B/1509